Speech Tips
with
Spunky Monkey

Lori Klisman Ellis, M.A., CCC-SLP
Lisa Sherbel M.A., CCC-SLP

illustrated by Lou Okell

Arkett Publishing
New Milford, Connecticut USA

Speech Tips with Spunky Monkey

Lori Klisman Ellis, M.A., CCC-SLP
Lisa Sherbel M.A., CCC-SLP

illustrated by Lou Okell

published by

ARKETT PUBLISHING
division of Arkettype
PO Box 36, Gaylordsville, CT 06755
860-350-4007 • Fax 860-355-3970
www.local-author.com

ISBN 978-1-0880-5123-8

Printed in USA

Dedication

This book is dedicated to approximately 3,720 speech and language students that we have worked with over our combined 67 years in both school and clinical settings. They helped us learn how to be experienced and patient therapists. Our students worked hard no matter what challenges/obstacles they faced. So thank you to each and everyone one of you! We hope many teachers, therapists and students get joy from this book.

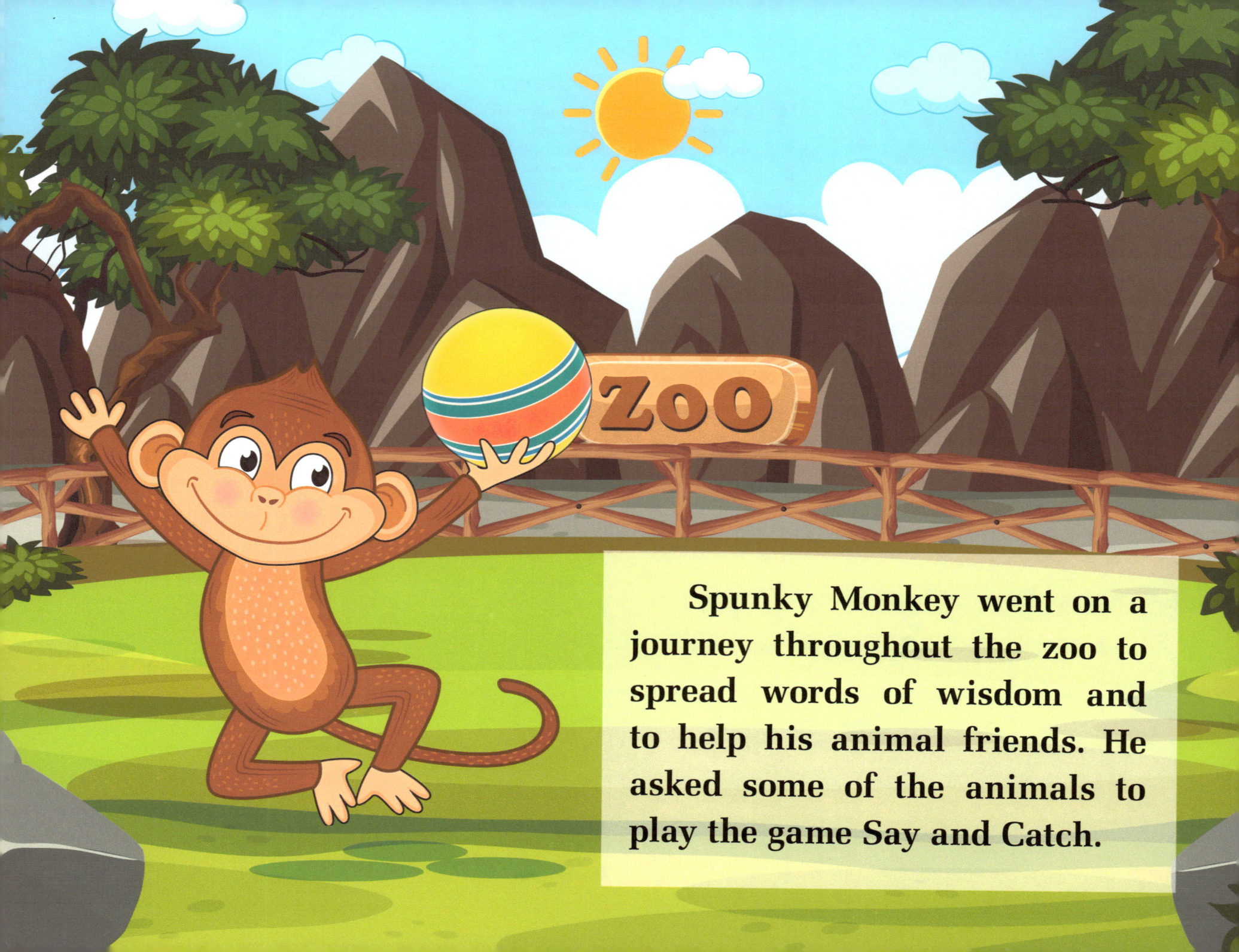

Spunky Monkey went on a journey throughout the zoo to spread words of wisdom and to help his animal friends. He asked some of the animals to play the game Say and Catch.

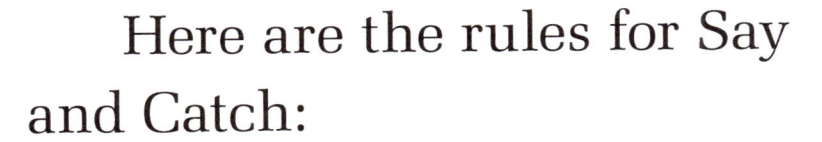

Here are the rules for Say and Catch:

Pick a category like fruits or toys. A ball is tossed in the air. Say something from the category before you catch the ball. If you can't catch the ball or come up with a name in the category you are out. "Who is ready to play?" asked Spunky Monkey.

Spunky saw Sophie the Snake and asked:
"Can you play Say and Catch with me today?"
"Nu, Nu, Nu, w…ay," stuttered Sophie. "I ca, ca, can't say the wwwwords with ease. I neeeeed help please."
"Talking is h-h-hard for me. I do better sli-sli-slithering up a tree."

Spunky said: "You know what, sometimes I stutter too, and it makes me feel blue. Just have fun and play. Can you do that for me today?"

"Take a breath and count to two. I won't interrupt or rush you. Throw the ball in the air. Say any fruit at all and catch the ball."

Sophie thought about what she wanted to say and used slow speech and said 'peeeeach'. "I did not think I could play, but your kindness is making this a special day."

Spunky said, "Sophie, can't you see, your friendship means a lot to me. Do you want to go for a walk to meet new friends and talk?"

"Y-y-y-yes I do," replied Sophie.

Spunky swung from tree to tree while Sophie slithered along the ground. They found their friend Alli the Alligator. Spunky asked if she wanted to play Say and Catch today.

"No way. I can't speak clearly or play. I can't thay the word even if it's heard. I'm tho different than you two and the words I can thay are very few," said Alli. "My speech thounds are not always precise, tho others ask me to thay the thame thing twice."

Spunky said, "You know what, sometimes I have a hard time speaking clearly too, and it makes me feel blue. Just have fun and play. Can you do that for me today? Throw the ball in the air. Then say any vegetable at all, and catch the ball."

SSSS ○○○

"Okay," said Alli, "Thelery."

"You almost got it!" said Spunky. "Watch me as I say 'celery'."

"That word has my favorite sound," stated Sophie. "Put your tongue behind your teeth, smile and stretch the /s/ sound until it is found.

Alli tried her best, "S..S..S..S Celery, I did it! I did not think I could play but your kindness is making this a special day."

Spunky said: "Alli, can't you see, your friendship means a lot to me."

"Do you want to go for a walk to meet new friends and talk?" asked Spunky.

"Yes," replied Alli.

Spunky, Sophie and Alli swung, crawled and swam up to Leo the Llama and asked, "Can you play the game Say and Catch with us today?" asked Spunky.

"How do you play?" asked Leo. "I get confused and never know what to say," Leo cried.

Spunky replied, "Trust me it's a fun game. Let's see how many toys we can name. Throw the ball in the air; name any toy at all and catch the ball.

"We will give you some choices. Now listen to our voices. We will name four things: bed, ball, lamp and rings."

Spunky said, "If you need more clues we will use pictures and you can't lose."

Leo gave it a lot of thought. He used pictures and words to help him learn, and he was able to take his turn. He announced confidently as he sat up tall, "It's a ball!"

"I did not think I could play, but your kindness is making this a special day," said Leo.

Spunky said: "You know what, sometimes I can't understand directions too, and it makes me feel blue. Leo, can't you see, your friendship means a lot to me."

Spunky said "Do you want to go for a walk and meet some new friends and talk?"

"Yes," replied Leo.

Spunky, Sophie, Alli and Leo found Huxley the Hippo cooling off in the water.

"Can you play the game Say and Catch with us today?" asked Spunky.

"Huh? What did you say? I can't hear, so how can I play?" asked Huxley.

Spunky spoke a little louder and said, "You know what, sometimes I have a hard time hearing too, and it makes me feel blue. Here are some easy tips. While I speak watch my face and lips. We can also use our hands to talk, just like we use our legs to walk."

"Hold up your thumb and pinky, and wiggle away. Now you signed you want to play. We will speak loud and clear, so have no fear. Say any clothes at all, before you catch the ball."

Spunky said "shirts"...

...while Alli said "socks"...

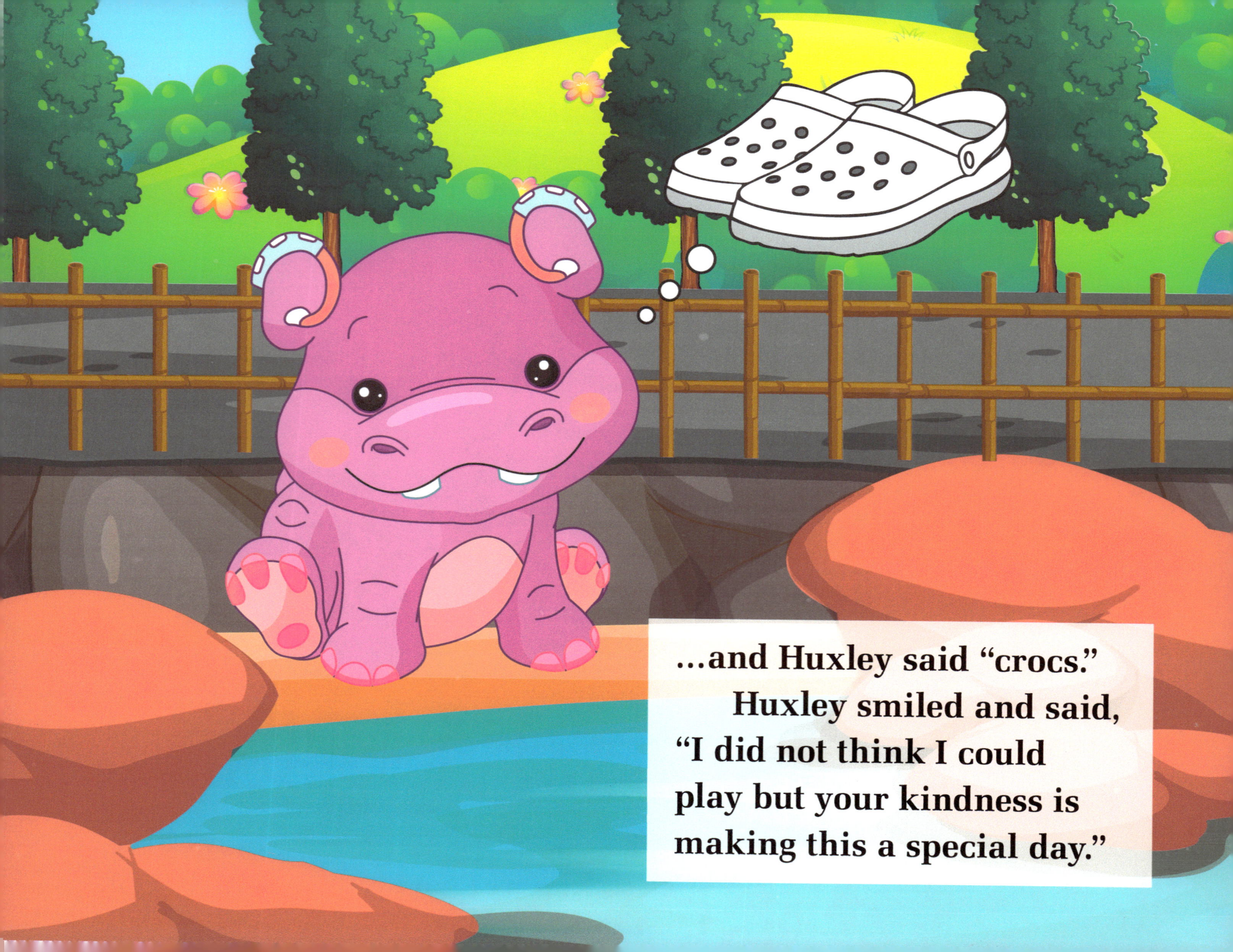

...and Huxley said "crocs."
Huxley smiled and said, "I did not think I could play but your kindness is making this a special day."

Spunky said: "Huxley, can't you see, your friendship means a lot to me."

"Do you want to go for a walk and meet new friends and talk?" asked Spunky.

Huxley nodded "yes."

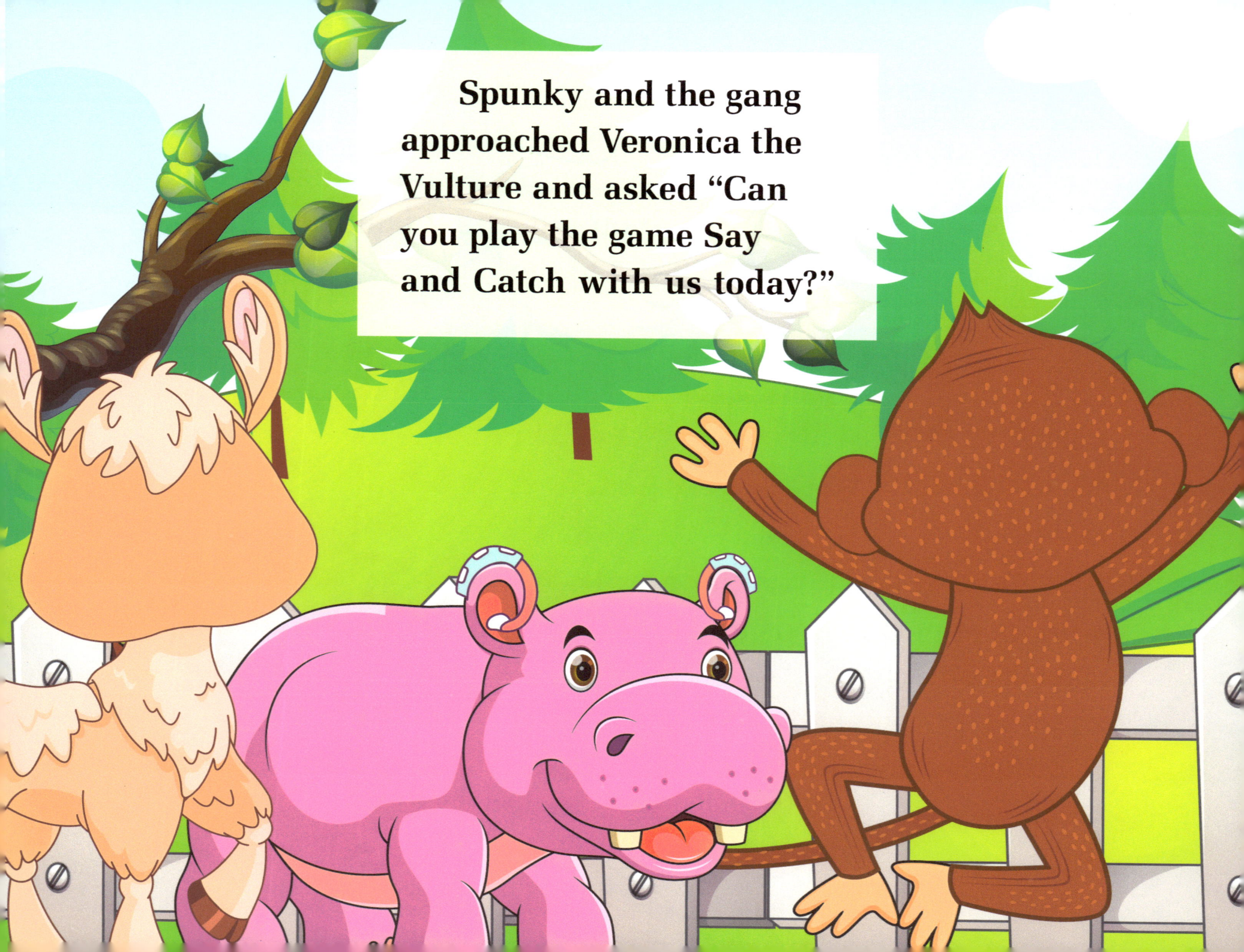

Spunky and the gang approached Veronica the Vulture and asked "Can you play the game Say and Catch with us today?"

She was screaming "No, but it's not my choice, it's due to my raspy voice. Sometimes my voice is fine, while other times it does not sound like mine. I am so different than all of you, and it makes me feel so blue."

Spunky said, "You know what, sometimes my voice is strained too, but it won't stop me from having fun in the zoo. Here are tips for your voice and any of these will be a good choice.

"Drink lots of water, go in the shower and breathe in the steam, and this should help your self-esteem."

"Yay," Veronica yelped.

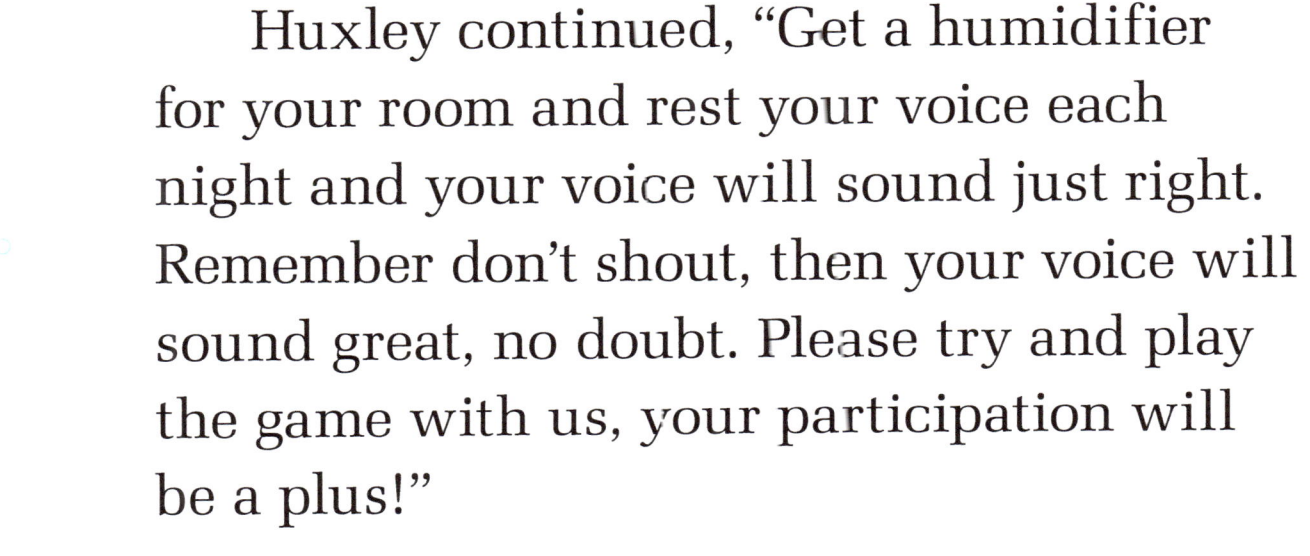

Huxley continued, "Get a humidifier for your room and rest your voice each night and your voice will sound just right. Remember don't shout, then your voice will sound great, no doubt. Please try and play the game with us, your participation will be a plus!"

"Toss the ball in the air, and name any animal at all, before you catch the ball."

Spunky said "monkey" while Leo said "llama"...

...and with an easy indoor voice Veronica said "snake." "Good job, give me a handshake," said Huxley.

Veronica proudly stated "I did not think I could play, but your kindness is making this a special day."

Spunky said "Veronica, can't you see, your friendship means a lot to me."

All the animals played near a tree, and said with glee, "Thanks Spunky for letting us play with you. We had fun and learned some speech tips too."

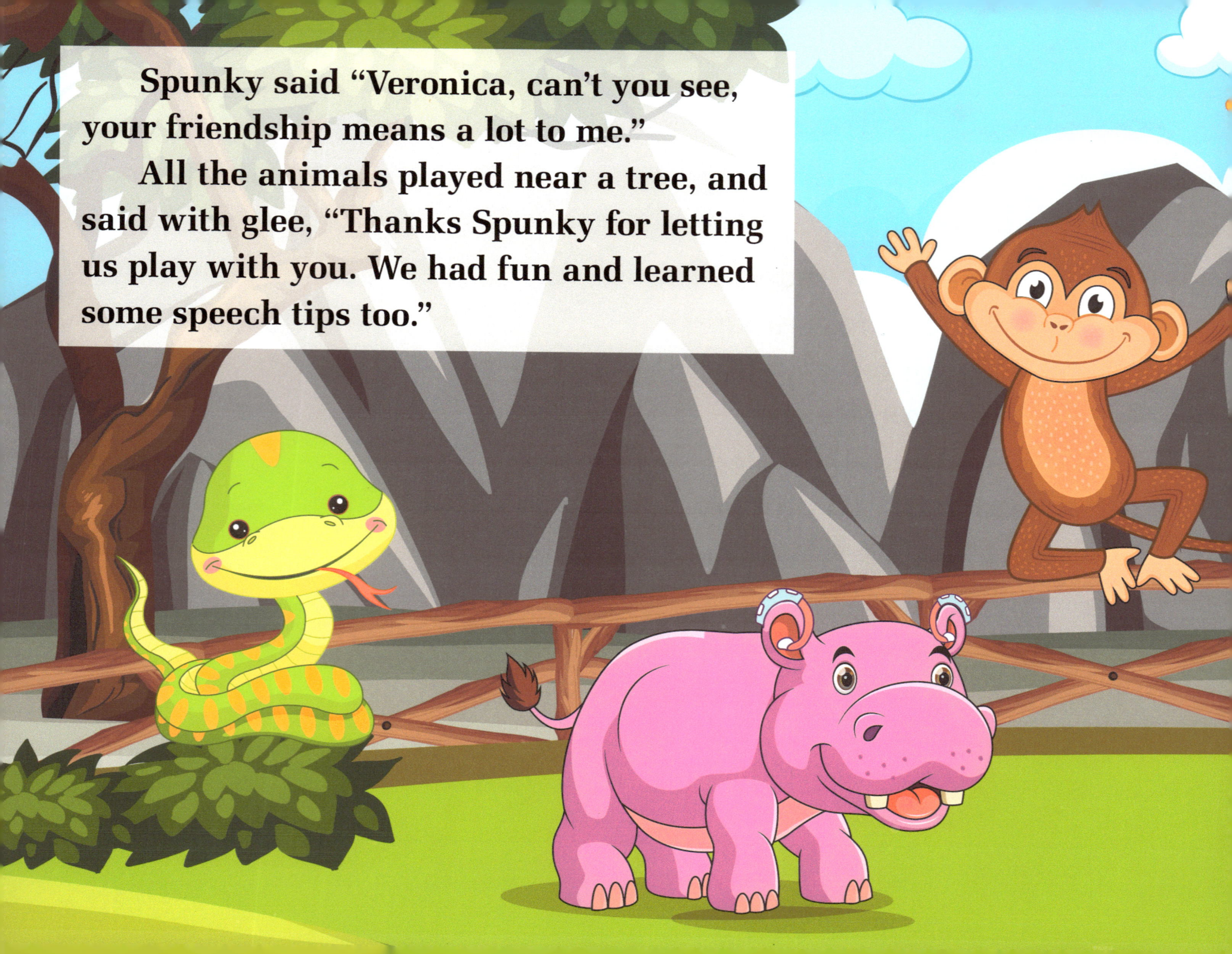

Do you know any friends/mammals just like these animals?
If so, do they struggle with hearing, talking or learning, or any other issues that are concerning?

If so, help is on the way so everyone can have a better day.

You can work with a speech and language pathologist in a clinic or in a school—they can be a very useful tool.

No one is perfect as we all know. Respecting each other will help us grow.

Companion Section

This section is for therapists/teachers/social workers and parents.

Match the animals with their speech tips.

A

Huxley the Hippo
is hard
of hearing

B

Alli the Alligator
has articulation
errors

C

Sophie
the Snake
is a stutterer

D

Leo the Llama
has difficulty with
language skills

E

Veronica the Vulture
has difficulty
with her voice

_____ Speak loudly

_____ Go in the shower and breathe in the steam

_____ Watch my face as I say these sounds

_____ Count to two or three before you speak

_____ Speak slowly

_____ Use sign language

_____ Put your tongue behind your teeth, smile, and make your /s/ sound

_____ Drink lots of water

_____ Use a humidifier

_____ Use pictures and/or have a choice of 4 words

_____ Don't interrupt others talking

_____ Don't rush people while they are talking

_____ Use a hearing aid

_____ No shouting

_____ Rest your voice

Companion Questions:

Stuttering:

- When a person stutters how do you think they feel?
- If a person stutters while talking to teachers or the principal do you think that would cause stress? If so, why?
- How do you think students who stutter feel speaking in class?
- If a person who stutters had to ask a stranger a question how do you think he/she would feel?
- What can they do to help their speech sound smoother?
- Have you ever had bumpy speech?
- Can you think of any problems a student may have because they stutter?
- Can you think of any tools that may help to reduce stuttering?

Voice disorders:

- How do you think students feel when their voice fades in and out, or their voice sounds harsh?
- What are some reactions one may get when people hear a raspy and loud voice?
- How do you think students do on a speaking assignment in class when their voice fades out?
- How do you think a student feels when they need to talk to a stranger with a loud, raspy voice?
- What can he do to help prevent this voice disorder?
- How would you feel if you were dealing with these voice issues?
- What are some problems a student may have if they have voice issues?

Language Disorders:

- What can a student do if they do not understand questions and/or assignment in school?
- How would you feel if your teacher gave you long directions that you did not understand?
- How would you feel if you did poorly on a test because you did not understand the directions?
- What are some problems a person may have due to difficulties understanding language concepts?

Articulation disorders:

- How would you feel if people could not understand your speech?
- What tips may help you speak clearer?
- What would you do if someone said you sound like a baby?
- What could you do if someone teased a student due to their articulation errors?
- How do you think they would feel giving a speech to the class if they could not say their /s/ and /r/ sounds?
- Do you think a student would have any problems due to articulation errors? If yes, what may be some of their problems?

Hearing Impairments:

- Have you ever had a hard time hearing your teacher give an assignment? If yes, what did you do about it?
- If you cannot hear a friend speaking to you, what would you say?
- What can you say to a teacher if he/she is speaking but not looking at you?
- What can you say to your parents if you feel you can't hear well?
- What are some tips you learned that can help someone with a hearing loss?
- How would you feel if you had to wear hearing aids?
- What do you think causes a hearing loss?
- What problems may students run into with a hearing loss?

Speech Tips with Spunky Monkey was created by certified speech and language therapists to reduce fear and anxiety when students initially start speech and language therapy. We hope you find this book as a fun and creative way to introduce different speech and language disorders. Attached is a companion section for therapists, teachers and/or parents.

About the Authors

Lori and Lisa have 67 years of combined speech and language therapy experience. Together they helped approximately 3,720 students with a variety of speech and language disorders in both school and clinical settings.

Lori Klisman Ellis has worked as a speech and language therapist for 36 years in Wayne county intermediate school district and Royal Oak school district. She is retired but still enjoys helping others. Lori and her husband Jeff have been married for 39 years and have two beautiful children, a daughter-in-law and a grandson. She enjoys writing books, spending time with friends and family, traveling and exercising.

Lisa Sherbel worked as a speech and language therapist for 31 years before retiring. She worked in the Macomb intermediate school district, various clinical settings, summer speech camps, and then spent the majority of her career working in the Walled Lake school district. Lisa has been married for 34 years. She and her husband Steve have a wonderful family that includes three children and a daughter-in-law. She enjoys spending time with her family and friends and doing creative projects.

Printed in the USA
CPSIA information can be obtained
at www.ICGtesting.com
JSHW041433060823

46005JS00003B/64